SQUARE IN THE EYE
a play in two acts by
JACK GELBER

GROVE PRESS, INC. NEW YORK

Library of Congress Catalog Card Number: 65-25826

First Printing 1966

Manufactured in the United States of America

TO MY PARENTS

*This work was begun while a
Guggenheim Fellow, 1963-64.*

The Performers

SQUARE IN THE EYE was first performed at the Theatre de Lys, New York City, on May 19, 1965. Produced by David Balding for The Establishment Theatre Company, Inc.; directed by Ben Shaktman; set design by Kim Swados; lighting by Jules Fisher; film by Leonard Glasser; and with the following cast in order of appearance:

ED STONE	*New York public school teacher and painter*	Philip Bruns
LUIS	*One of Ed's students*	José Perez
SANDY STONE	*Ed's wife*	Carol Rossen
AL JAFFE	*A painter*	Gene Rupert
JANE JAFFE	*Al's recently divorced wife*	Dixie Marquis
BILL, JR.	*Sandy's son from her first marriage* . . .	Alan Howard
SARAH	*Ed and Sandy's little girl*	Kerrie Lynn
HY BECKER	*Sandy's father* . . .	Alfred Dennis
SALLY BECKER	*Sandy's mother* . .	Eda Reiss Merin
DOC		Conrad Bain

ACT ONE

Scene One

The Stone's workroom. Early November, 1962.

ED *enters from auditorium in the bow-tie bright manner of a stand-up comedian.*

ED:

My mother always wanted me to be a doctor. Secretly I, too, wanted to become a doctor. Actually, I'm not Jewish. My wife Sandy is. She and I have lied about that to her orthodox parents. I love it. I mean playing the Jew. What pain! Let's face it! If I had been Jewish, I would have become a doctor. Instead I have the rare privilege of teaching art to delinquents in the New York public school system and I suffer. How I suffer! You couldn't believe the misery I'm in. If my mad mother had been Jewish, I would be cleaning up a fortune and have a hell of a lot of time for painting pictures. If I were a doctor, just for an example, my bill to anyone of you would be astronomical. I'd wipe you out just on an office visit. That's what happened to me. My mother was shoved into confinement, which drove her nuts and cleaned me out. Of course, you might have health insurance which would mean only one generation would get wiped out. If you're lucky, your children will live without the hospital bill. But that's being middle class. I have nothing against the middle class. For Christ's sake I'm middle class. Freud was middle class. Marx was middle class. My mother was middle class. Don't think that I'm any different. Just because I painted a few thousand pictures doesn't change the old socio-economic outlook. As a matter of plain fact just last week a guy offered me a job as a stand-up comedian in the Bronx two nights a week. How middle class can you get? It's just that being middle class creates certain hang-ups. Certain expensive problems like insurance. My father warned me about insurance. He was always warning me about insurance. And that's how he died, without any insurance. (*Chokes himself on his own tie*)

Sandy wants to move. I don't want to move into another apartment. Every day she screams at breakfast she wants to move. What's wrong with the lower West Side. It's as safe as the upper West Side. Well, not as clean as the East Sixties. And, this morning, Sandy was bugging me to buy one of those fag suits. Oh god. What do I need to buy labor-saving devices for? Who ever heard of a garbage disposal unit in a cold-water flat? And that's not the half of it! I can't even afford a divorce! I've been trying to save up enough money for a divorce for years. And every damn year hospital bills or summer vacation plans or something or other turns up and zap! there goes the bankbook. I've tried to get Sandy to go to work and help out. She thinks its ridiculous for her to go to all that trouble just to get a trip to Nevada or Mexico. Oh, she wouldn't mind going herself but who wants the kids along? I'm not going to take care of them. Her mother couldn't be bothered. That's exactly the point. A Governor Rockefeller can send his old lady out of state for a quickie uncontested divorce and not do anything to change the stupid law. It's all a lot of crap. You may think I resent my wife. I don't really. We just beat the hell out of each other. I don't have enough time to paint pictures and I don't have a decent studio. And that makes me mad. How long can you go over the same arguments? I'll tell you: forever. And what makes it worse, it's all bickering. Like this morning. I can't even remember how it started. It's not Sandy's fault that we have two children. I mean, Sarah is our little girl and Bill, Jr. is Sandy's boy from her first marriage. She was married to a dentist. Her mother and father loved him like a son. You know I didn't marry her for her brains. Come on, let's face it, she's a wonderful piece. I dress her up in black lace and nylons or whatever fetish I'm hung up on

and schtupe her. It's heaven. What's the matter?
You haven't read a sex manual lately? Come on,
let's face it, it's better than spilling your seed on
the ground.

Sound of school bell, noisy kids, transistor radios.

MOVIE

LONG SHOT: *High school kids leaving school; coming
out of a door and going down steps.*

MEDIUM SHOT: *Matched cut. Action as above.*

CLOSE-UP: *Matched action cut as above.*

*The two side screen surfaces are stills of the same kids
with the sound track continuing.*

MEDIUM SHOT: *Ed Stone and Luis coming out of the
door and down the steps. From the sound track now
there are disparaging remarks of the students to Ed and
Luis. Words such as "brown nose . . . Luis is kissing ass
. . . Mr. Stone eats it . . . ," etcetera. Luis has a transistor
radio.*

Let's stop here for a moment's explanation.

FREEZE FRAME: *Ed Stone and Luis duck.*

*The two side stage surfaces have other stills, showing
the kids catcalling and/or throwing things.*

You may wonder why I'm ducking. The reason is very simple. There is a Dr. Brown's Cherry Soda bottle and it is aimed at my skull.

START ACTION: *Ed and Luis walk away.*

Next to me is Luis. It's Friday and I've invited Luis over vaguely hoping to have some friends hear him read poems. Sandy won't like my not warning her about Luis, but I hope she won't be too bugged. What I like about him is that he adores me. It's that simple.

CUT *to subway interior: Wide-angle shot of Luis. He is holding up his transistor radio and on the cue—*

We are on our way to my place. I'd like to give him a view of something other than the East Bronx. He is one of my more talented students, and I don't have many.

Luis picks up his Superman comic book.

Actually he is a much better poet than painter.

WIPE *or* DISSOLVE *or* WHIP PAN *to subway entrance exterior.*

CUT *to Jane.*

That's Jane Jaafe.

CUT *to Jane, Ed, Luis talking. No lip synchronization.*

Divorce looks very good on you, Jane. I've always wanted to ball her. Whew! She and my oldest friend, Al, have just gotten divorced and sneaky Ed, that's me, sees

CUT *to Jane.* CLOSE-UP.

an opportunity to finally consummate that long-time passion. Who's getting the studio, Jane?

MEDIUM SHOT, *Jane and Luis. Jane (voice over): "What are you doing with that young Moor?"*

I hope that explains why I never do get to make it with Jane Jaafe. I like aggressive women, but that broad terrifies me.

CUT *to Ed and Luis walking away. Ed stops.*

Jane, why don't you come over for dinner and we'll listen to some of Luis' poems?

CLOSE-UP *of Jane. Jane (voice over): "Balls!"*

Translated that means she will buy dessert and come over.

CUT *to Ed and Luis: They are walking around the corner.*

CUT *to building.*

That's my home.

ZOOM SHOT: *exterior of building or from a* MEDIUM LONG SHOT, *dolly to doorway and into darkness.*

That is my wife, Sandy.

Light on SANDY *and* AL *on set in action.* SANDY *wearing an apron.*

Say something, Sandy.

SANDY:

I want to move.

ED:

Don't be a smart-ass. Where's Al? He's so shy, my buddy Al. Let me finish with my introductions.

A colored still of Bill, Jr. and Sarah on left panel.

That's Bill, Jr., Sandy's kid from her first marriage, and my little girl, Sarah.

On right panel, a still of Hy and Sally Becker.

My terribly nice in-laws, Hy and Sally Becker.

AL:

(*His shoes off*)
We're gonna be in for it.

SANDY:

Why?

AL:

Well, isn't it obvious? When Ed comes in, he'll think we've been a-making it.

SANDY:

Jesus Christ, face it, Al. You're impotent. Nothing's ever happened. If Ed asks me anything, we'll just tell him you're impotent.

AL:

Don't get me angry! How do you like that—now

I'm getting hot. Holy cow. Listen, this is ridiculous.
Do you think we have time to make it right now?

SANDY:

You really do want to get caught with your pants
down. Don't worry. You're safe. My analyst told
me about types like you.

AL:

Your analyst *talks* to you? How much do you pay
him?

SANDY:

Look, Al, you're no friend of mine. You're supposed
to be Ed's buddy. Just because you're divorced now
you think you're free to bug me. If you have anything to say, say it to him. I'm busy. I've got work
to do.
(*Exits to kitchen*)

AL:

Sandy?

Pause.
Sandy?

SANDY *enters*.

Pause.
Why are you wearing that apron? You deviant!

SANDY:

I've got to get the children's supper ready and
begin ours. You are staying for dinner aren't you?

I've got to get this house clean just in case my mother and father pull a surprise visit on Friday night which is quite like them. I've got to finish that article on women painters of the late forties for Art News and I must attend a meeting to prevent a nuclear holocaust.

AL:

You gonna save the world! When does Ed come home from school?

SANDY:

He's probably listening at the door.

AL:

Boy, I'm lucky. You are a paranoiac. No wonder you have to see an analyst.

SANDY:

Well, you see one too.

AL:

That's different.

SANDY:

Pish posh Charlie.

AL:

I can afford it.

SANDY:

Go scr—

AL:

I don't need to go.

SANDY:

That, of course, explains everything.

AL:

Am I glad I'm not married anymore. When I'm around you I feel rotten.

SANDY:

I wish we could get out of this apartment.

AL:

You know what they say: One always gets the apartment one deserves. I think you're trying to block the apartment.

SANDY:

Stop your garbage theorizing.

AL:

I have a real function. You may be a hell of a lot smarter than I am and so forth and so on, but you just haven't got any idea who you are. Neither does Ed when you're right down to it.

SANDY:

You leave Ed out of this. You're a mean, arrogant, and selfish oaf who just happened to get lucky with your last show of paintings.

AL:

I just wanted you to admit that you're attracted to me all the more for my arrogance, aren't you?

SANDY:

I could really slug Jane for letting you off so easily.

If I were getting a divorce from you I'd squeeze money out of you. I'd make you the sorriest creature—

AL:

(*Sweetly but knowing it's killing her*)
You can't squeeze blood—wait a minute, Sandy. I'm the first person in the world to admit what a sweet and wonderful person Jane is. I just couldn't work. I couldn't function. As a matter of fact I've advised Ed to get a divorce from you no matter what it costs. He's got to give up teaching and really start painting again.

SANDY:

He could do it anytime he wanted. I'm not stopping him. However, we are not discussing my husband. I am telling you that you are a needlessly cruel, stupid—

AL:

Say any more and I'll be forced to rape you.

ED *and* LUIS *enter.*

Is that your game?

SANDY:

I'm writing to the President. What are you going to tell him?

ED:

I hate to break in on you like this, but this is my castle. Sandy, this is Luis. That poet I've told you

about. This is my wife, Sandy. She was probably
writing the President. That's why the house is a
mess. Isn't that so? I thought we'd invite a few
people up and have Luis read some of his poems.
Where are the kids? Hey, here's our first guest.
Hi, Al. This is Luis,
(*Interrupting* LUIS *from responding*)
and wait until you hear him sing.

SANDY:

That's very sweet of you. Imagine helping the
underprivileged by having them perform for your
friends. How much are you charging?

ED:

Come off it. I just can't wait. Luis, do the one you
did today. The one called Down.

SANDY:

Come on, don't do that to him.

ED:

Come on yourself, Sandy. I practice what you
preach.

LUIS:

Down, down, down. Down, down. Down, down.

*Repeat with taped music in background and slides of
Luis playing musical instruments on side panels.*

Face down. Downtown. We go down. Downtown.
Believe when I tell you. It's safer to go down than
dooooooo. Your face is smooth but your crotch is—

SANDY:

Hold it!

Music out. Fade images.

Did you write that, Luis?

LUIS:

Not exactly, Mrs. Stone. I'm sorry—

SANDY:

I see. Ed, I think it's absolutely disgusting.

ED:

Oh yeah.

SANDY:

It's a piece of juvenile garbage.

ED:

You really think so?

SANDY:

Goddammit, Charlie. I told you so. It makes me cringe with disgust.

LUIS:

Don't blame it all on Mr. Stone. I did write some of it. It's not all his fault.

ED:

That's wonderful. What else did you think about it?

SANDY:

Luis must be having a ball with his girl friend.

LUIS:

I know you can't tell, but I'm blushing now.

ED:

Is that right? This is just the best thing that's happened all day. All week in fact. Great way to start the weekend. Hey! Al! I say, I saw Jane on the street with her twenty-four hour Juarez suntan.

AL:

Are you speaking of the woman I love. The young lady I've just divorced?

ED:

None other. How can you tell me you love her?

AL:

Listen, Ed. Get these bourgeois notions out of your head. I love Jane. She's one of the finest—

ED:

Why is it that some years you are unbearable? You can explain yourself when she shows up with dessert.

AL:

Never had anything but dessert when I was married.

SANDY:

Isn't that a strange coincidence. I've invited Al to dinner, too.

ED:

That's wonderful.

SANDY:

Just because Al sold every painting in his one-man show doesn't mean you have to put him down, Ed, baby.

ED:

You shut up.

SANDY:

What are you going to do? Beat me?

ED:

I'll wait for the children to come home before I try any physical stuff. We might as well let them in on any skull bashing. I wouldn't want to neglect their educations. I'll pass on what my father showed me.

AL:

Just because you're not feeling like company doesn't mean I'm going to pass up dinner.

LUIS:

Mr. Stone has a tremendous influence on all of us, Mrs. Stone. You know he's the only teacher that fights back. He's down. Bad. Very bad, man.

SANDY:

I'm not a man and he's positively evil.
(*To* ED)
Can't we stop this?

AL:

Listen, Ed. I think Jane is a wonderful person. You don't have to feel we're enemies just because we're divorced. Jane and I never argued. You know that, don't you? I don't mean that you and Sandy argue all the time. It's just that Jane and I never raised our voices to each other. It's all my fault that it didn't work out.

ED:

I suppose it's easier when there aren't any children involved.

AL:

I don't know. I wouldn't be a slave to my children. Not that you guys are. No, no, I didn't mean—well, look, lots of famous men don't have children. George Washington, I was reading about—

ED:

(*Groans*)
I understand. Luis, did you know my old pal Al Jaafe is a wonderful and successful painter and one day I'll lead the class on an invasion downtown to his studio and you'll see how a real painter works.

AL:

Don't let him fool you, Looie, I just had a couple of breaks. Really, I'm only getting what I want. And, if it makes you feel any better, I'm only at the beginning.

LUIS:

Man, if you're at the beginning where am I?

ED:

I could use a beer.

AL:

I guess painting classes are like therapy only cheaper.

ED:

What are you talking about?

AL:

Art, man, art.

SANDY:

Bullshit.

ED:

Not in front of my students.

AL:

I wasn't being personal. I'm never personal. You guys are always carrying a chip. You take things, oh, I don't know—

SANDY:

(*Interrupts*)
I'm weary of attacks on psychoanalysis.

ED:

I don't follow.

AL:

Anyway, Looie, you got yourself one hell of a painting teacher. Believe me—

ED:

Thanks for the endorsement, however, I'd like a beer and no nonsense.

AL:

Teaching painting ain't easy.

ED:

Stop playing the cornball.

AL:

You think it's easy. It takes years of practice to say the wrong thing at the right time.

SANDY:

No one's perfect.

AL:

I know you do a good job with your kids. I know enough to realize that kids like little Loo-ie here don't get invited to their teacher's apartments very often.

SANDY:

Not unless there's some evil purpose—

ED:

Thanks a million. I'd rather have a wife that went out and worked while I painted all day.

AL:

Don't kid yourself. If you wanted that badly enough you would do it.

ED:

I've got plans.

SANDY:

Where do I fit in that scheme?
(*Interrupting* AL)
Ed paints as many pictures as you, Charlie.

ED:

That's not what Al's talking about. It da quality, honey. I don't have those collectors lined up.

AL:

I don't put down teaching. I'd like to have me some disciples. They could run about sweeping the floor and mixing things. Man, I'd love it.

LUIS:

Could I go home now?

ED:

Do you realize that this is only November. I'm not going to make it. Lord, help me! Just help me get to the summer. I've got to learn how to coast. Glide. That's it. Coast through the year. Concentrate on the galleries. That's it. Make friends. Yeah. Be really naive and obnoxious. That's the winning ticket. Ah, don't forget a touch of undiluted arrogance. Don't talk sensible, don't respond—not really respond, just let them get their jollies off. And then, let's see, first there's the big exhibition. Then the money and the waiting lists of patrons. Paint each picture to order. Of course, one must change dealers or at least threaten to. The divorce follows and your wife gets most of the dough you make anyway. I wonder if it really is worth holding out to the summer so that I can paint all those fine pictures just to go through pure agony.

SANDY:

I think we could all use a drink now.

AL:

I don't see how anyone can actually teach painting.

The very most you could hope for is that they pick up some of your genius by just talking to you while they're sweeping up or mixing paint. Then the little buggers can get it by osmosis.

ED:

Get what? Syphilis?

SANDY:

Ed!

ED:

I can see the Board of Education getting a report on your classroom activities.

AL:

It's not as farfetched as you make it out. I've heard you talking about the stupidity of the public school system and I never thought I'd hear you defend it.

LUIS:

Mr. Stone?

ED:

All right, I'm a coward. Let's face it, I'm never going to be able to send my kids out to work. After all, Al, baby, it is entirely possible that my contribution to the wonderful world of painting will not be worth the effort. What if all this is just self-indulgence?

AL:

What about sending Sandy to work?

SANDY:

I'm untalented. I can't type and I take lousy short-hand. I'm not going to start a career and compete with you big boys. Are you nuts.

God, I wish I could do something to make money and then all this bickering would end once and for all.

(*Exits*)

ED:

Oh, we'd find something else to argue about.

AL:

Of course, that's just what I've been telling you: you're always raising your voice.

ED:

Al, this just isn't your year with me. First of all mind your own business. You know that I can't bear any friend of mine becoming a success.

AL:

I have a theory about success—

ED:

Why don't I have a beer or a drink or something? (*Exits*)

AL:
Pause.

Uh, Ed and I are old friends.

Pause.

He's just a little upset about my selling out my one-man show. You know, it's hard to accept your friend's success.

Pause.

That's not really it. You know what really bugs him? I don't need a chick anymore.

LUIS *stands up.*

No, man, no, no. Listen, you got a girl friend?

LUIS:

No, sir. I mean, yes, sir.

AL:

For Christ's sake call me Al. I have a theory about sex, Loo-ie.

LUIS *takes a step back.*

Hey, did you do these?
(AL *picks up a folder of drawings*)

LUIS:

By hand, sir.

AL:

Very clever. Yeah, they swing, Loo-ie. They really do.

LUIS:

Mr. Stone didn't like them.

AL:

Pause.

Do you have a girl friend? Oh, I asked you that already, didn't I? Do you make it with her? Oh, man, you don't have to hide it. It's no shame. I've got a reason asking. Nothing personal. I want to see if my theory will hold up.

Pause.

Anyway, all there is to sex is friction. Like two sticks rubbing together.

LUIS *backs up again.*

Logically you don't need women.

LUIS *takes another step.*

Masturbation.

LUIS:

Pause.

It softens the brain.

AL:

Don't be silly. The chicks really don't know what to make of you if you don't come on and you're not a faggot.

LUIS:

You're putting me on.

AL:

No, no, I'm serious.

LUIS:

You're a grown man. As old as my father. Everyone knows that jacking off saps your energy. You'll go nuts.

AL:

Did you ever stop to consider that it requires no fuss, no bother and generally speaking it's clean. Right?

LUIS:

You've got to be putting me on.

Pause.

I think you're right about one thing. You can't let 'em ever know you want it or they won't give it to you.

Enter ED *and* SANDY *with glasses and beer and a coke, for* LUIS. ED *is humming the song* LUIS *sang.*

AL:

You know Jane is really a good little girl. When you are less involved with her you can see just how really nice a chick she is.

ED:

I don't want to talk about it.

SANDY:

I don't want to talk about it.

AL:

I want to clear up a few things. You all think that I'm rich? That dough was spent the next day. Besides, I'm willing to pay alimony. I've nothing against that. Jane deserves every break. You're deluding yourself if you think my worldly success has anything to do with our breaking up. Jane knew that we couldn't make it with me strung out, unable to work, irritable, miserable to live with in every way.

SANDY:

It's just a tiny bit selfish, sweetie, just a tiny bit.

AL:

Golly, I'm sorry about being selfish. I think men rule the world. I guess it makes it tough on women. Jane needed special attention and I couldn't give it to her.

ED:

(*To* AL)
Can't you talk about something else?
(*To* SANDY)
Who should we call over tonight?

AL:

Pause.

You know we were never in love.

ED *and* SANDY *groan.*

Really, we didn't even dig balling anymore. We didn't need each other. You two are masochists. Come on, face it, don't tell me any differently, I've known you for years. You've never made it any secret. Screaming, yelling, hitting each other. Hell, man, I'm the one who is civilized. I'm not a cannibal.

ED:

Are you finished? As long as Jane is coming over, we might as well have a party . . .

SANDY:

(*Interrupting*)
I'd like Al to go on. We women will go to any length in satisfying our need for punishment. And then what happened?

AL:

I like clearing the air. I think it's good for me.

ED:

Yeah, but what about us?

SANDY:

No, Ed, let him go on and dig as deep as he can.

LUIS:

Sir?

ED:

You can have a beer if you want.

LUIS:

No, sir, this'll be all right.

AL:

Why can't he stop calling us sir and mister? It makes me feel old and decrepit.

ED:

I prefer it the way it is. Do you mind?

AL:

It's so damn undemocratic. Not that I care much

for democracy. You know that. You're the one
that's always putting me down for having aristo-
cratic ideas and now the shoe is on the other foot.

ED:

I don't wear storm trooper boots. Jesus, don't tell
me you're going to give us a lecture on Greek
culture!

AL:

(*Mock Yiddish*)
Dolly, so why should I tell you anything?

ED:

God, your Yiddish stinks. You know I never
realized that. Your success may be attributed to
your very bad Yiddish accent. Anyone can do it
well, but to do very badly—ah, there's the rub. No
wonder all those collectors are delighted with you.
You've got them all lined up. They're knocking
down the walls to get on your list. It's a perfect
touch for an absolutely ingratiating politician. Yet
you have problems finishing work, don't you, Al?
Can't get it out fast enough, huh, buddy?

AL:

I've never denied it. I do have work problems.
What's wrong with making small talk with friends?
You make it sound dirty. Man, you're somewhere
else. I can't help it if your talents don't include a
minimum of social grace. What do you do with
those kids all day? What do you have to say to your
fellow teachers? Your brain is going soft.

LUIS *laughs*.

ED:

There's nothing wrong with making friends. I find it unrelated to talent.

AL:

So do I.

SANDY:

I'm happy to hear you fellows agree on something.

AL:

I'm likeable and you're not. It's that simple.

ED:

What's your secret?

AL:

Flexibility. You've got to learn to stay loose under press—

ED:

Oh, I thought you had some special underpainting technique. Makes your pictures last forever. Glow in the dark . . .

AL:

(*Interrupts*)
Very funny. I can't help it if you're inflexible.

ED:

Contradicting yourself again?
(*To* SANDY)
Did you buy a one pound tube of titanium white? I think I'll work this weekend.

SANDY:

I've been running around all day. I didn't have time to buy anything.

AL:

No, not at all. Everything changes so fast that one thing is true one minute and the complete opposite is true the next. You take everything so personally.

ED:

Oh, you mean I should be more objective, less abstract.
(*To* SANDY)
What were you doing all day?

AL:

I didn't tell you to become an abstract expressionist.

SANDY:

Who said anything about that?

AL:

I can't be blamed because my kind of painting is popular right now. I don't make the trends. Actually, I admire you for sticking to your guns and doing your kind of painting.

ED:

I wish I could do my kind of painting this weekend.

AL:

Man, I'm not sure that I would have had the guts. Really. I mean I just happen to paint in a more popular style. It's not my fault.

SANDY:

That certainly is not a fault.

ED:

(*To* SANDY)
I'll call you when I need you.
(*To* AL)
I seem to bring out the best arguments in you.
(*To* SANDY)
Another drink, please.

AL:

I've had enough for now.

SANDY:

I'm not going to be spoken to as a servant.

ED:

Why not? You're not married to a dentist anymore.

SANDY:

If we're going to have a lot of people over I think someone will have to go out for more booze.

ED:

What's that supposed to mean? You know we're broke.

SANDY:

I didn't mean—

ED:

(*Not waiting for an answer*)
I work hard all day. Goddammit! Don't needle me. Go peddle your ass if you want more money.

I can invite anyone I want. And if there's nothing
to drink I'll let them worry about it. So fuck off!

AL:

What do you think?

ED:

About what?

AL:

About my theory.

ED:

It stinks.

AL:

Shall I try another one?

SANDY:

You're going out of your mind. I wasn't putting
you down.

AL:

They're all the same to me. Art can't be explained
so what's the difference how many theories I make
up.

ED:

When I blow, I really blow. I'm sorry.

Offstage noises of JANE JAFFE, BILL, JR., *and* SARAH.

Enter the little devils.

AL:

You know as much as I admire little Loo-ie's work,

you've got to admit that art is not therapy although it might be therapeutic.

JANE, BILL, JR., *and* SARAH *rush in from auditorium;* SARAH *jumps into* ED'S *arms.*

JANE:

Hello, Al. Nice seeing you again. Hi, Sandy . . . Ed . . .

LUIS:

Luis.

JANE:

Hello, Luis.

BILL, JR.:

Sandy, will you pay attention to me. I want you to tell Jane she may not kiss me any more. I'm really upset. I really am. Let's face it. I'm not exactly a child anymore. I'll . . . I . . .

AL:

Jane! You should be ashamed of yourself. Robbing the cradle. The least you could have done is pick up a stranger.

ED:

It's a comfort to know that you two never argued. Luis, these are my children. Sarah and Billy.

AL:

You don't call that arguing, do you? We never argued about anything important.

BILL, JR.:

I saw your show, Al. I liked it very much. Heard you sold out the first day. Wow!

AL:

Thanks. I didn't know your parents took you to the gallery.

BILL, JR.:

They didn't. I went myself.

AL:

Hey! That's a real compliment.

BILL, JR.:

I do have some criticisms.

ED:

Now Billy—

BILL, JR.:

Why not? We're all grown up. Someone ought to tell him.

SANDY:

You grow up and shut up!

BILL, JR.:

Someone ought to tell Al that he's too derivative.

ED:

Is that all? Whew!

BILL, JR.:

Oh, you think I'd tell him what I overheard you saying.

AL:

Why don't you let the fellow speak? You and your democracy. Billy, you tell me what you think. Not what anyone else tells you.

BILL, JR.:

It's evident that your ideas are nothing more than an amalgam of de Kooning and Kline. That's just for a start.

AL:

Billy, I'm not in the least offended. See? When you grow up I hope you follow my example in taking criticism well. It generally takes a big person to do that.

JANE:

That's a laugh.

AL:

Gee, Jane, you ought to see some of Loo-ie's drawings.

JANE:

Stop pimping.

AL:

That's what I am. I've always been a pimp. My earliest memory is putting mother up for sale.

LUIS *laughs*.

BILL, JR.:

I'm going to my room and do some constructive homework.

(*Exits*)

ED:

God, twelve-year-olds are obnoxious.

AL:

It's only because it's your kid. Let him alone. He'll be all right. What did you tell him about my show?

SARAH:

When do we eat? Oh, daddy seven years old is all right, isn't it?

JANE:

I suppose you think I was overdoing it with Billy? Well, maybe I was but it wasn't intentional. Sorry.

SANDY:

Don't be silly. I didn't say anything.

JANE:

Well, maybe I need to break out a little. Whhooo-peee! Right, Luis, baby. Come on cutie—smile.

ED:

You're looking very well, Jane.

JANE:

Why don't we leave all these squares to their dull fate and cut out of here. I'll take you home and give you a bath . . . anything. What's your idea of luxury? Want to become a painter? Honey, I'm an expert at making boys into painters. I've got this studio I've just inherited.

ED:

You're not being fair. Stop it, Jane. This kid doesn't know what's happening. You're talking all around him. He doesn't even know whether to take you seriously or not.

AL:

She's serious.

JANE:

I'm serious. I'm a serious person.

ED:

I know there's a perfect answer. Somehow it's slipped out of my head and is on its way to limbo. I'm not going to spend the next hour trying to cap every clever remark you two dream up. I'm tired. I'm wasted from putting up with teen-age fantasies and I'd like to eat.

SANDY:

It's a little early.

ED:

Do I have to eat by the clock? Goddammit! If I'm hungry I want to eat.

SANDY:

You'll have to wait for the children to eat, unless you want to eat with them.

ED:

I didn't ask to bargain.

JANE:

You're wrong, you know.

ED:

What?

JANE:

It's entirely possible your brain has sent a distorted signal to your stomach. In fact I'd bet on it. I think you are rebelling against the idea of eating with all of us thereby precip—

ED:

You've been living with that fellow too long. Whew! You got out just in time.

SANDY:

You can't put me down and expect me to cook dinner for everyone.

ED:

How do I teach a class after being humiliated? Have another beer, Luis. How you doing, kid?

LUIS:

My mother—

ED:

We'll call her.

AL:

I'll make chili for everyone.

JANE:

Oh, great. Al's chili is the greatest.

SARAH:

I don't like chili.

SANDY:

I'm stuck.

AL:

That's what all chicks say. If a man cooks he's competing.

HY *and* SALLY BECKER *burst in the room from auditorium.*

HY:

Oh, you've got company.

SANDY:

Daddy, come back. We don't have company.

ED:

Hi, hi, Hy. How's the drugstore business?

HY:

A friend of yours was in the store.

SALLY:

What ugly furniture!
(*Winces at set*)
Sandy, you must forgive me I'm so nervous. But this is no way to live, darling.
(*Notices* LUIS *and gasps*)

AL:

(*Offers* SALLY *a chair*)
I think your parents must have been great in vaudeville.

SALLY:

Thank you. I can see you have manners.

SANDY:

What's bugging you two?

HY:

I won't discuss it. No, I refuse to say another word. There's a right and wrong and I'll stick to it even if there's someone who won't.

SALLY:

It's unclean. What happened to the little horses I gave you?

BILL, JR.:

(*Entering*)

Who were the white roses and which side were the red ones?

SALLY:

You got a cousin Rose. Where is the vase I gave you—the one with the roses? It was very expensive.

HY:

I won't be goaded into an argument in front of my grandchildren.

(*To* LUIS)

Who are you?

ED:

He's one of my students if it's any business of yours.

SANDY:

There's only one solution. Shoot the children.

HY:

Don't talk about business. Rich, you're not. A professional man you're not. A host, never. A liar—yes.

ED:

Come off it, Hy. What's eating you?

BILL, JR.:

(*To* LUIS)

You mean you're older than me and don't know which side was the red roses and which the white?

ED:

Shut up, Billy.

HY:

I'll bet you'd hit him if we weren't here.

SANDY:

What are you saying?

HY:

It's no secret that Billy takes after his father.

SALLY:

You could have fixed it up again, Sandy. Bill is really a wonderful professional man. I went to see him yesterday. What an office—just like a living room.

SANDY:

Mother, this is insane.

SARAH:

Why is everyone shouting?
(*Starts to cry*)

ED:

Why don't you kids go do your homework?

HY:

Listen to the way he talks.

ED:

If you don't tell me what this is all about I'll get violent.

BILL, JR.:

My father wouldn't use threats of violence.

ED:

Shut up!

BILL, JR.:

I think you have been unduly influenced by your students.

SALLY:

You wouldn't dare.

ED:

Why not?

SANDY:

Don't threaten my mother. You're always using threats of physical violence. Maybe you are taking on the switch-blade mentality.

AL:

> (*To* ED)
> Need any help? I'm an expert iconoclast.

ED:

> No, thanks. I'm not stopping until I find out what's happening.

JANE:

> The mistake came in not feeding him. That always pacifies them. A nice corned beef sandwich for a nice Jewish boy.

HY:

> That's it! You've broken her heart. You liar. You're not Jewish.

A thunderclap over the loudspeaker.

ED:

> (*Singing, dancing, raving*)
> I'm not Jewish. He's not Jewish. She's not Jewish. We're not Jewish. You're not Jewish. Jewish. Jewish. Jewish.

SANDY:

> Of course Ed's not Jewish. I was only trying to protect you.

SALLY:

> It's not too late. I called Bill before coming over.

SANDY:

> Bill's remarried.

ED:

I'm getting out of here.

SANDY:

You can't go now.

ED:

I know myself. I'll do something we'll both regret.
I can't stand this noise or your parents.

SANDY:

How am I going to—

ED:

You can cope. You always cope. I'll see you later.
(*Exits into auditorium*)

SARAH:

(*Still crying*)
You promised to take me to the zoo tomorrow.

SALLY:

She has a temper just like her father. That's right.
Run out.

ED:

(*Off-stage*)
Don't wait up for me.

JANE:

I'll come with you.

SANDY:

(*To* JANE)
You better keep your head.

SALLY:

See, he ran out on you. They're all the same.

SANDY:

He didn't run out on me. What's all the noise about?

HY:

You deceived us!

SANDY:

Come on, I'll make you some tea.

SALLY:

(*Last to exit into kitchen*)
It's this life he's making you lead. This place!

SANDY *takes her parents into the kitchen.*

LUIS:

What am I supposed to do?

JANE:

Don't worry, honey. We'll find something to keep you busy.

Lights out. Music begins. LUIS *in spotlight. Set changed during song.*

LUIS:

(*With taped musical accompaniment*)
Scared, I am scared, so scared that I can't move
Can't move, cause I'm scared if I don't
and scared if I do.

Shoe talk—poor, love talk—hate
I'm not right—
What they trying to say?

Scared, I am scared, so scared that I can't move.
Can't move, can't move, can't move.

LUIS *exits through auditorium.*

Lights out.

JANE *and* AL *exit during blackout.*

Scene Two

A medical conference room. A funeral parlor. A chapel.

Three days later.

ED *enters through the auditorium.*

DOC, HY, *and* SALLY *enter from stage entrance.*

DOC:

Let me reassure you that we have some of the finest brains—minds in the country working on your daughter, wife. I have explained what we have attempted to do in the last three days with your daughter, wife and now I'd like to spell out the costly difficulties. This, as you doubtlessly guessed, is the brain.

HY:

(*Interrupting*)

You know there are fourteen doctors working on her.

SALLY:

Fourteen! How lucky can you get? What money can't buy.

DOC *coughs.*

HY:

Are you listening, schtunk?

DOC *coughs.*

ED:

Yeah, I'm listening.

SALLY:

You know who's to blame. If you hadn't run out on Sandy, maybe . . .

DOC *coughs.*

ED:

I didn't run out.

SALLY:

(*To* ED)
Sssh!
(*To* HY)
I think the doctor has a cough.

DOC *performs an elaborate ritual of lighting a cigarette.*

HY:

Who's going to pay for all these specialists?

SALLY:

Didn't even have added coverage.

DOC:

(*Raps the pointer*)
There are many possibilities and I have every reason to believe that your daughter, wife will make a rapid recovery. Dr. Kopeck is a fine surgeon.

ED:

Surgeon?

DOC:

Yes, surgeon. He was called in two and one-half hours ago and I have been led to believe he is in the operating room at this moment.

ED:

Would you please explain? I didn't know Sandy was being operated on.

SALLY:

How could you know—

DOC:

I'm sorry but I have other patients to attend.

HY:

Explain already. We're not idiots. Please, explain.

DOC:

Mrs. Stein was brought into the intensive care unit at 9:30 this morning.

Quick light cue for brain movie. Either the curtain is

*used as the screen or if possible it should be opened and
a screen backstage used*

Cranio cerebral trauma may be divided according to
the nature of the injury of the skull into three
groups. Closed head injuries may further be divided
into three categories. And not to complicate mat-
ters we shall only consider cerebral edema.

ED:

(*Interrupts*)
Hey! Who gave permission for my wife to be operated on?

DOC:

Why, her father I guess. I don't believe you were
around, son.

ED:

It's illegal. You can't do that.

HY:

It's done. It's my daughter. I'm a professional man
and I know what's best for my daughter. Although
to tell you the truth I didn't know she was being
operated on.

SALLY:

Where were you? With some tsatskey? You know,
Hy, this doctor is a doll much more Sandy's type.

Movie of brain, or electroencephalogram.

DOC:

Please, this is serious. Here is a picture of the electroencephalogram showing the depression of cortical activity. The real danger sign of course was when the cerebrospinal fluid proved to be clear and colorless. This is an indication that there is complication of cerebral edema. It must have been quite a fall.

SALLY:

Oh! I'm going to faint.

HY:

What fall?

DOC:

Perhaps we ought to continue this later.

SALLY:

No, no. It's my daughter.

DOC:

If you don't mind I have other business.

HY:

We'll wait.

ED:

Send word about Sandy.

DOC *exits.*

HY:

Why do you always interrupt? Keep that lousy mouth shut.

SALLY:

Don't act the big shot. You're only a druggist. Big shot. In those days all you had to do was pass a test and you were a pharmacist. I know you blame me. You've always blamed me for having to quit school. But you don't fool me. You don't understand what Dr. Apfel is saying either.

HY:

What kind of health insurance does the Board of Education provide? You aren't capable. What kind of man runs out on his wife?

SALLY:

So, where is he?

HY:

Who?

SALLY:

I don't trust him.

HY:

Well, what kind of insurance is it? Blue Cross? Blue Shield? Major Medical?

ED *finds Sandy's medical chart.*

SALLY:

I was thinking of that doctor.

HY:

He's costing a fortune.

SALLY:

He smokes with a cough.

Enter DOC.

Oh, hello, Dr. Apfel. There's something wrong. A mother knows.

DOC:

I'd like to speak to you alone, Mr. Stein.

SALLY:

My daughter's dead.
(*Wails*)
I know it. You don't want to break the news to me
. . . I know it.
(*Sobs*)

DOC:

Yes, I'm sorry.

HY:

Oh, god, how could this happen, she was so young.

DOC:

I think you had better take care of your wife.

ED:

I want to know what happened to Sandy.

HY:

You're not entitled to explanations only the bills.

ED:

I still want to know what happened.

DOC:

Extradural hemorrhage is the most fatal of complications. We did all we could.

ED:

Oh yeah! What? For example.

DOC:

You are understandably upset.

ED:

Don't be so goddamned understanding and tell me
what happened.

HY:

I won't pay a dime.

DOC:

I'm sorry you know we don't work on results.

ED:

(*Holding Sandy's medical chart behind him*)
What happened to my wife.

DOC:

The body has no mechanism for the absorption of
an extradural hemorrhage.

ED:

Yeh?

DOC:

Probably there was a tear in the wall, Mr. Stein.

ED:

Go on.

DOC:

We had extensive laboratory proof that surgical
intervention was absolutely necessary.

ED:

So?

DOC:

I didn't wait for a complete finding.

ED:

Why not?

DOC:

I thought you deserved to know as quickly as possible. If you could excuse me now I've other patients who need my help and perhaps some other time I can go into the details if you like.

ED:

No, I want to hear more now. It's comforting. Keep talking.

DOC:

Usually the hematoma is quite large.

ED:

Yeah.

DOC:

And very often over the convexity of the hemisphere in the middle fossa.

ED:

Yeah.

DOC:

The clotted blood remained in the epidural space as a tumor until it was removed by the operation,

Mr. Stein. I want one thing made very clear, Mr. Stein. The operation was a complete success.

ED:

Dammit! My name is Stone not Stein. I know I look Jewish.

SALLY:

He looks Jewish.

ED:

My name is Stone. You get it?

DOC:

I'm sorry, Mr. Stone. I have so many patients. I've been up more hours than I care to think about. You're not going to hold a slip of the tongue—

ED:

You say the operation was successful?

DOC:

What's your wife's name?

HY:

What kind of professional man are you?

SALLY:

Sandra Stone.

DOC:

Not Sandra Stein?

HY:

I'll sue. I'll sue you, the hospital, my heart won't take this—

DOC:

Wait a minute. Let's be calm.

ED:

You have a bizarre sense of humor.

DOC:

I must have a report on her somewhere.

SALLY:
Sandra forgive me. I thought you were dead.

ED:

I hope you don't tell us that Sandy's operation was
a success too?

DOC:

Don't badger me!

ED *throws Sandy's chart on the table.*

DOC:

Here it is . . .
(*Laughs*)
I'm sorry, but your wife is dead.

ED:

Did I say you had a bizarre sense of humor?

DOC:

She died of—

ED:

Come on, you can't expect us to believe you now.

DOC:

I'm sorry, your wife is dead. She died of peritonitis about two hours ago.

HY:

She's been dead while we were talking?

ED:

I just don't believe you. Hy and Sally can believe you but I think you are an imposter.

SALLY:

He's not very professional.

ED:

I want to know every detail. How else can I believe you? I've got to know every complication in her medical history.

SALLY:

Finally, Satan, I agree with you.

DOC:

I'm not an internist.

ED *laughs*.

HY:

What's so funny?

ED:

Mistakes don't count.

SALLY:

Mistakes don't count is right.

ED:

Well, Doc, did my wife know she was dying?

DOC:

I wasn't with her.

SALLY:

What a thing to ask. Oi. Morbid.

DOC:

I'm sure she was comfortable.

HY *quietly sobs.*

ED:

I didn't ask if she was comfortable. I asked if she knew she was dying. I'm not letting you leave here without a full medical explanation.

SALLY:

Something I can tell my friends when they ask how it happened. Something.

HY:

All you want is for it to be an educated disease.

DOC:

(*Picks up book and reads*)
Organisms most commonly encountered are normal inhabitants of the gastrointestinal tract, chiefly the gram-negative coliform bacteria and streptococci as well as Ps. aeruginosa, A. aerogenes and staphylococci. Organisms may reach the peritonem by the following routes, one, inflammation of or perfora-

tion of the gastrointestinal tract as a result of appendicitis, peptic ulcer, Meckel's diverticulitis, diverticulitis neoplasm, volvulus, mensenteric vascular occlusion, intussusception, foreign body, cholecystitis, pancreatitis, and typhoid fever. Then—

SALLY:

How can I say, "My daughter died of a foreign body"?

DOC:

Lights fading.

Remember she could have had an infection of the genital tract or—and perhaps it's worth noting that had she survived I would have recommended psychiatric treatment.

Light and music transition.

DOC *is leading* ED, SALLY, *and* HY *to another part of the stage where several caskets are arranged.*

I know the strain you're under. Leave everything to us. Remember hundreds visit us each year and actually, we have earned our reputation.

SALLY:

The courts wouldn't let him keep the children. Would that be justice? Never.

HY:

Naturally, Bill, Jr. will go back with his father. What are we going to do about our Sarah?

ED:

Sarah is staying with me.

SALLY:

Blackmailer! We're going to take you to court. You
can't get away with this. You're an unfit father.
You remember what happened to Ruby's kid?

HY:

This isn't the time for arguments.

DOC:

Yes, I think we can start here. Worldly business
first. It's up to you what kind of funeral you want
to give your recently departed loved one. We
merely are here to aid in carrying out your decision.
This particular gorgeous piece of workmanship is
something everyone will be talking about for a
long time to come.

HY:

You should have had more insurance.

SALLY:

Now, Hy. Let's get what we are here for. It's not
nice to discuss our private business in front of him.

DOC:

Walnut, plush red velvet interior, brass fittings, old
world charm. The departed one can be made up in
her favorite party clothes carrying a bunch of her
favorite flowers. Then her guests can approach her
in a less somber mood more like a tea—

HY:

Flowers? This isn't going to be orthodox?

SALLY:

Why should it? Sandy wasn't thinking about that when she married?

HY:

Don't you understand? That doesn't matter.

ED:

How much?

DOC:

What?

ED:

How much is it going to cost?

DOC:

I was going to wait until we got back to the office before discussing the financial arrangements. How many guests will be invited?

HY:

Oh, no. Oh, no. We're not going to go cheap on this. No, no, no. This is my daughter. I don't care what it costs. We're going to have a funeral.

DOC:

Now I can agree with that.

SALLY:

If only you had more insurance money.

ED:

Do you have a pine box? Something simple. Sandy would have liked something simple.

HY:

My daughter wanted only the best.

ED:

Sometimes the simple—

HY:

Just don't worry about it. I'll take on the burden, as usual. Sit down already. You make me nervous.

DOC:

Why don't we all sit down for a moment. We must be very tired indeed.

HY:

What else have you?

DOC:

We have for your further inspection several outstanding examples of final resting places. I suggest that we might delay the decision on the casket. First, let me give you some idea of the different types of gatherings we can produce given a little time.

Light cue and stills or movies. First picture is of Egyptian pyramid. Image at first partially covered and grows bigger as speech progresses.

Our most opulent affair. A funeral fit for a Pharaoh. We need to hire a few extras to dress it properly.

SALLY:

Pharaoh, phooy.

DOC:

This is a little

Image is reduced to blackness.

ostentatious for your needs but I thought you might get a kick out of seeing a really big one. Here's another grand gathering.

Shots of bridal film.

Humm! We have the bridal ensemble. That's where we dress the loved one in the garments of her wedding. Her guests are, of course, in their appropriate costumes.

ED:

Nooooo . . .

DOC:

It was merely a suggestion.

HY:

You're not paying for anything, big shot.

Newsreel shots of New York garment industry funeral.

DOC:

For the big city dweller . . . The ever-popular labor leader procession. Our casting is impeccable. You know we fool a lot of people. These things are easier to stage than most of the general public think.

SALLY:

Remember Izzie's funeral? Oh, what a thing! What a beautiful casket!

DOC:

Our distinguished citizen's parade—

Movie of small motorcade.

SALLY:

I like it already.

DOC:

We can stop traffic on Fifth Avenue or Riverside Drive, if you prefer. Around town with police escort and cortege. This is a particularly nice time of year for a funeral. I think we can promise you a big turn out.

SALLY:

Go no further.

Freeze frame on the last shot of the motorcade.

HY:

This is a class funeral.

Dissolve image. Muzak music in background while JANE, AL, BILL, JR., SARAH *and* LUIS *enter.*

SALLY:

Where are the flowers?

HY:

But you were the one who complained that we should keep it kosher.

SALLY:

> I can't change my mind?

DOC:

> (*Puts on skull cap*)
> Of course, we can all have a change of heart. A little religion shouldn't hurt anyone.

HY:

> Some things you shouldn't change your mind about.

ED:

> That's all right, you can always divorce her.

DOC:

> Please. Pleased I am to be here.

Pause.

KADDISH

Yisgadal v'yiskadash Sh'mey Rabbo. Be'ol'mo deevro Chiroosey, ve'yamlich Malchoosey, Be'chayeychoen u'vyoemeychoen, u'vchayey De'chol Baiss Yisroel. Ba' agolo uvizman koreev, v'imroo Omaine.

Extolled and hallowed be the name of God throughout the world which he has created. May his Kingdom be established speedily and without delay during your lifetime and during the life of all the House of Israel. And say you all amen.

Another long pause.

> I see you when you are married and I see you when one of your loved ones dies. I am with you when

your fears exert their deepest pull. So you do not remember the many times in history that the courts were corrupt, public life venal, priests filthy, despair, as today, everywhere. Remember and turn to your faith. You will pray. The dead don't pray. It is for the living to invoke my prayer. We are the ones to ask forgiveness and mercy for our suffering—for suffer we will.

SALLY *wails*.

Beloved friends, beloved relations. I am able to say something about Sandra Stone because I know her for many years. I married her.

SALLY:
He's not Jewish!
(*Sobs*)

HY:
It's all right. Go on.

DOC:
Sandra Stone worked very hard as a mother, daughter, wife and not least for love between men. A sensitive girl, one who appreciated her husband's painting and the rich meaning of life in all visual crafts, Sandra was at the beginning of a marvelous life. If you ask "why?" I cannot tell you. Faith and belief will only help you. It won't answer that question.

BILL, JR.:
She wasn't kosher.

ED:

Be quiet, son.

SARAH:

She was a lousy cook anyway.

ED:

True, all too true.

HY:

Have you no respect for the dead?

SALLY:

Have you no respect for the dead?

DOC:

My point is this: here was a young mother who was interested in civil rights. Although Sandra was young she worked on many committees to defend her beliefs in the innate goodness of man. Bow down thine ear, O Lord, hear me: for I am poor and needy. Preserve my soul: for I am holy: O thou my God, save thy servant that trusteth in thee. Be merciful unto me, O Lord; for I cry unto thee daily. We will pray.

Bows his head. Repeats the Kaddish in Hebrew and then translation with males chanting with him.

ED:

(*During chant*)
Who gave him the bullshit about being a civil rights worker?

HY:

How do I know? She did something like that didn't

she? Against the bomb or something like that. She always was fighting? She should have been a boy.

ED:

(*To* SARAH)
We've got to get out of here.

SALLY:

Murderer—running out again. You Nazi!

(*Bites* BILL, JR. *who screams*)

ED *and* SARAH *exit through auditorium. Everyone else out through stage exit after prayer. Lights fade and music is heard.*

Scene Three

A hotel ballroom. Six weeks later.

Music turns gay. DOC *and stage hands dressed as waiters change the set.*

ED *enters from auditorium. He is wearing wedding clothes.*

ED:

This is the greatest! Hi, Sam! Hello, Bob! Jimmy baby, glad you made it in from the Bronx for my wedding. Still teaching school? That's not for me.

SARAH *enters.* ED *lets out a cowboy yell.*

Sarah, you remember Doris? She lost her husband a couple of years back. Couldn't get over it. Poor soul! Maybe we'll be an example, huh, baby?

SARAH:

Now you're talking like Grandma.

ED:

Not my mother. You mean Sandy's. Mine's nuts, you know that. You know what they all say. Just as easy to marry a rich girl as a poor one. Yeah. Hey, look who's showed up. Hi, Al.

AL:

Ed, I never thought I'd see you happy again.

ED:

Hell, life goes on. You're doing okay yourself. Glad you could make it, buddy.

AL:

In six weeks. You're a fast worker.

ED:

It wasn't easy. Let's face it! She's rich and she's beautiful. She's got everything. I wouldn't go so far as to say Sandy did me a favor, but you are right when you say everything's coming my way. (*Goes into audience, thinking he's spotted a friend*) Oh, you must be one of my wife's guests. Hi, Sally! Hi, Hy! This is truly wonderful.
(*Kisses them*)
Wonderful! Sarah, say hello to Grandma and Grandpa.

SARAH:

Isn't this fun?

HY:

Congratulations, Ed.
(*Stuffs a white envelope in* ED'*s pocket*)
We hear she's a nice girl who happens to have a
lot of money so you won't need that, but we thought
you'd appreciate the gesture. Right?

SALLY:

I know Sarah is in good hands now.

DOC:

Everything all right over here?

SALLY:

Everything is beautiful.

HY:

It's fine.

ED:

Very chic, don't you think?
(*Turning to* JANE *and* LUIS)
Hey, guys, I heard the news. Hearty congratula-
tions! You kids are just made for one another. It's
lucky you grabbed her before I had the chance,
Lou-ie, baby.

JANE:

Stop your kidding. And don't go congratulating
us yet. You're the one that's getting married.

LUIS:

I'm going to try my hardest . . .

ED:

Of course you will.

Enter BILL, JR.

How lucky can a guy get? All his old friends are here to celebrate his new-found happiness. Great to see you!

BILL, JR.:

(*Hands* ED *a white envelope*)
My father sends his regards.

ED:

Thank you very much, Billy.

JANE:

Hey, Ed. I know Sandy would have approved. Now Sarah will have a family and you'll get some work done. Life can sure change quickly. I know it did after Al and I broke up.

ED:

How's about one of them great songs, Lou-is?

LUIS:

I can't sing anymore.

ED:

Come on, you can't mean that.

JANE:

It's true, he can't sing.

AL:

You're going to have plenty of time to paint now. Of course, that's dangerous. I know.

ED:

Don't you worry, buddy boy. So I don't paint. Big deal. Or I do. That's my choice now. I'll straighten that out soon enough. By the way, I didn't mean half of those things I said to you . . . when was that? A thousand years ago.

AL:

That's all right, Ed. I got mine my way and you're getting yours in the only way you know how. You'll probably be successful.

ED:

Have I changed or did I always feel this way and didn't know it? Well, it doesn't matter anymore. I've had it revealed to me before I died so I'm thankful.

AL:

It's all for art's sake anyway, isn't it? You may not know it, but you're much more obsessive about painting than I am.

DOC:

Come on, boys, enough of this chitter chatter. We've got a wedding on our hands.

ED:

Howdy, Doc.

JANE:

Oh, oh. Ed's beginning to affect a Western accent just like Al's.

SALLY:

You see what a good time is?

HY:

You should open your eyes.

DOC:

Let's get this over with before the bride changes her mind.

Music. Everyone begins to exit, leaving ED *and* SARAH.

ED:

(*To* SARAH)
Come on, Sarah. Go show the grandparents a little smile.

SARAH:

Yippee!
(*Exits*)

Music stops abruptly. ED *steps forward.*

ED:

I had to do it this way, I couldn't make it alone.
(*Exits*)

Music resumes then fades.

INTERMISSION NOTE

A few minutes before second act begins, a photo of Sandy is shown on one of the side panels. Photo off when second act begins.

ACT TWO

Scene One

The Stone's workroom. Back in early November, four days after the funeral.

ED *enters from auditorium, wearing a light raincoat.*

ED:

(*Begins speaking as though dead*)
Let's face it. You never know. You just never know. The day before yesterday at the funeral they were calling me a murderer and they're just stupid enough to call the stupid cops and they might stupidly arrest me. All right. I admit it. Take me away. Not only did I kill her and then not mourn which you must admit is only a normal reaction. Not only did I do that—I admit kissing her. So she was dead. What are they going to hang on me? A sentence of life imprisonment? Christ, they're always smooching with dead people in movies. You like to identify? Well, I was just fooling, I didn't kiss any dead broad. I just said that to expose every necrophiliac member of the community. Come on,

73

I'm sure you've got the courage of your own per-
versities. No? Anyway, Sandy's mother and father
are being very clever with lawyers threatening to
take Sarah away from me. You see? I can say
"Sandy."
(*Tries to sing*)
Sandy, Sandy, Schmandy, Mandy. Hey, all you
paranoids, there's a way to read a relationship between Negroes and Jews in that. If you listen
closely. No? Oh, well, you can't win them all. You
can't use Gestapo techniques against the Gestapo.
Isn't that right, Laydies and Gentlemen? You won't
be able to tell the difference between the fake and
the real. Of course, that turns out to be no problem
at all. It's all real. Right? Kee-rect. So I say to
the little kid. Kid, I certainly contributed to mom's
death. Sandy was a nervous woman. I only abetted
in making her a hell of a lot more nervous. Take a
good look at her mother and father. Now, being
nervous, your mom's lower tract got infected.
Thousands of germs attacked it. That should be
clear. And then her colon was pierced by one of
them which in turn caused massive infection of the
peritoneum. Sarah, you'll just have to grow up
and become a doctor. What? Yes, sweetie, it is
very true that I wasn't around when Mommy got
sick. No, Grandpa is wrong when he said that
daddy was with another lady all that time. Not
that I wouldn't have been had I the opportunity.
What's so terrible about that? As a matter of fact,

Grandpa better fork over some dough and pretty fast or I'm going to make his little Sarah into a shiksa. I've got the law on me side. For once. No one can take my daughter away from me. That's my meal ticket, my love. I made some mistakes like walking out. But you can't put me in jail for that. That's what they are threatening. Oh, God, I've done everything I'm supposed to.

(*Weeps*)

DOC *enters from auditorium.*

DOC:

I've come about the ad.

ED:

What?

DOC:

Your name Stone?

ED:

Yeah.

DOC:

Well, didn't you advertise that you had some handmade women's suits?

ED:

Oh, yeah. Come in. Sit down. Sit down. I did do that. Yes. I suppose you can guess why?

DOC:

No. No, I don't know why. I thought I'd—

ED:

My wife died and won't be needing them.

DOC:

No, I didn't know anything about that.

ED:

I'm sorry. I thought I was being funny.

DOC:

Oh, your wife didn't die. I get it.
(*Laughs*)

ED:

No, she died all right. Forget it. Want a drink?

DOC:

No, no, I don't think so. I'd—

ED:

I need a drink. Let's not be antisocial over a stinking drink. God, there's nothing to drink. I'm sorry.

DOC:

That's all right, I didn't want one.

Pause.

Sorry about your wife. I don't know about the clothes now.

ED:

The clothes are the very best. You buying for your wife? A terrific buy, really, she'll be very pleased.

DOC:

Can I see them?

ED:

What do you need to see them for? You're going
to buy them anyway.

DOC:

What makes you so—

ED:

Come off it! My wife's just died. You're going to
deny food for my little girl? Take the goddamn
money and get out. We don't need you.

DOC:

I only asked to see the suits.

ED:

Okay. I'll go along with that.
(*Gets suits*)

DOC:

They . . . uh, don't seem to be the latest style.

ED:

They're hand made in Europe. Feel this material.
A classic cut.

DOC:

But the colors are—

ED:

Give me ten bucks apiece and I'll let them go.

DOC:

I don't know—

ED:

I said give me ten bucks apiece—

DOC:

Okay, okay. I've got to get my wallet out.
(*Hands him the money*)
I guess I better go now.

ED:

Don't you want the suits?

DOC:

Oh, yeah.

ED:

(*Stopping* DOC)
So you think you can buy your way out.
(*Laughs*)
Not on your life. I know guys like you. A few bucks
down and you think it's all over.

DOC:

Just because your wife died doesn't mean you can
push me around. I—

ED:

You know about my wife dying? Sure, you know
who started it? Well? I'll tell you. It was the faggots.

DOC:

The—

ED:

Faggots. You see, there was this guy, Harvey, that
my wife and I knew. We knew him for years and
years and I never said more than two or three words
to him but my wife had long talks with him. She

complained to him, mostly. Girl talk. You know. Well, you know, he couldn't mind his own business. He goes into my father-in-law's drugstore and drops a bomb which was enough to kill my wife.

DOC:

What happened to your father-in-law?

ED:

He's all right.

DOC:

What's your friend's name?

ED:

I'll kill him. If he were here I'd kill him.

DOC:

Thanks for the suits. They're very nice.

ED:

If you think I'm nuts remember I've got the money.

DOC:

So long.

ED:

Remember I'd kill him if he were here.

DOC:

It's unreasonable, but I understand. So long.

ED:

Of course it's unreasonable.

DOC *exits through auditorium.*

I'm unreasonable. But, I've got to strike while the iron's hot. If I wait to bludgeon them for what I need it'll be too late. And it's perfectly normal for me to be going through all the various anxieties about money, the children, the future. If they ask how I can carry on business so soon after Sandy's death, I'll pretend I'm merely in shock. I've got them coming and going.

JANE *enters from auditorium.*

I've got to use that kid more. Show her around. Yeah, take her to the galleries, show up for dinner with her. Don't push it too hard or I'll have the courts after me.

JANE:

For what?

ED:

You've scared the hell out of me.

JANE:

I thought I better come over and look after you. I didn't think anyone else would remember.

ED:

I'm not exactly helpless, but—

JANE:

Of course, I came because, you know, old Jane, she's just got to help the sick, the wounded and the underprivileged. You hardly have to ask and she's there.

ED:

What have you got in mind?

JANE:

I know you. You probably are just callous enough to want to screw me right here and now.

ED:

I—

JANE:

Don't bother to deny it. Where's Sarah?

ED:

At school.

JANE:

School?

ED:

Why not?

JANE:

Isn't it a little early? I guess not. I think you were right. You generally are.

ED:

I knew you felt that way. Sarah's all right. She needs to have a routine. Great assurance, routine.

JANE:

I would have sent her for other reasons. But then it's not my child.

ED:

Well, now you still have time to have children of your own.

JANE:

Not likely.

ED:

Oh, these things are all so mysterious. It gets me sick.

JANE:

Me too. Really, it's not all that mysterious. You know, I've never known you to be in the least bit interested.

ED:

Purely as a stud.

JANE:

What?

ED:

A service. That's how I desired you. I'd think to myself. If I can arrange the time, I'll just jump in the sack with her and remind her how much having a child means to her. And fertile old Ed will do the job if there's a job to be done.

JANE:

You know all you had to do was to give me that little speech and I'd drop right into your arms.

ED:

Maybe I didn't for that very reason.

JANE:

I don't think so. I think you didn't do it because you were afraid.

Pause.

You're afraid now.

Pause.

Listen, if you need anything—use me, cleaning, washing, anything. I'll give you a hand. I'd better be going now.
(*Exits*)

ED:

(*Arranges some of his paintings*)
I suppose it would have been infinitely more interesting to have bastard kids all over the place. That's it! Goddammit, I need to exhibit largesse. I've got to do it.

Pause.

I'm too tight, in everything—no wonder I can't work. All I can think of is Sandy's face and ass. What do I want to do that for all over again?
You can't do the same thing over and over.

AL *enters from auditorium.*

Oh, some can. Some make a career out of doing the same thing over and over. And God help them if they change. Out they go! Maybe I'm not cut out to break new ground.

AL:

Jesus, I'd of thought you'd be the last guy in the world to feel sorry for yourself.

ED:

I must be going nuts. I didn't hear you come in.

AL:

That sort of proves my point. Stop moping around and get to work.

ED:

Who invited you here?

AL:

Ho. Ho. Ho. Very funny, Ed. I'm sorry. What did you want me to bring? Flowers? Did I interrupt you? Were you painting already?

ED:

I doubt if it's any of your business.

AL:

I'm not going to be fooled by your hostility. I know it's only in reaction to your old lady dying. I've got this theory. By the way, have you got a cup of coffee? Say, I'll bet you're so helpless you've forgotten how to make coffee. Instant will do although you know I despise it—that's about as much sympathy as you're going to get from me, buddy. As I was saying, I've got this theory about you— hey, when did you do that one?

ED:

Two summers ago. Go on and say your piece.

AL:

I just don't believe in pampering. Pampering only

delays things. I say come right out and say what's on your mind before you make a thing of it. Don't you agree?

ED:

No.

AL:

Sandy kicked off and that's that. You can't do anything about it. I suppose you will roll around in bed for a week or two lolling in your new found freedom but then you'll wake up and thank Sandy for setting you free.

ED:

What makes you think I didn't plan it?

AL:

Plan what? Sandy's death?

ED:

Sure, man, why not? I dig little girls.

AL:

I never thought of that.

ED:

Besides, I'm not free.

AL:

Won't Bill, Jr. go live with his father? And, Sarah. Surely you can get the Beckers to look after her— after you've done your dirty deed. You wouldn't dare. You're putting me on. I never know whether you're putting me on or not.

ED:

I am keeping my daughter.

AL:

Must be out of a guilty conscience.

Pause.

I'm sitting down. Or, is that a taboo?

ED:

You can't expect me to keep up with social amenities. What taboo? You nut.

AL:

There's some Indians in South America who believe that when one of your friends dies you shouldn't sit down for three days.

ED:

Horseshit.

AL:

Of course, you're right. How did you know? Dear me! You mean I didn't have to admit that one? I'm always getting trapped on the insignificant lies —never on the big ones. Isn't that the way things always go? I mean, you should know.

ED:

What's that supposed to mean?

AL:

Your non-secret was let out of the bag, wasn't it? I mean the Beckers finally exposed you for the goy you are.

ED:

I don't know how it came to be a secret.

AL:

How'd they find out?

ED:

Harvey Bates.

AL:

Who's he?

ED:

You should remember him. I was under the impression Harvey Bates was a very special friend of yours.

Pause.

Come on, a couple of years ago he was conning painters through some co-operative.

AL:

The guy with a bad complexion.

ED:

Red hair. Nasal voice.

AL:

Anyone you don't like has got to have a nasal voice. Sure, I joined up with him. Nothing ever came of it. Oh, I know why you don't like him. He felt up Sandy in front of a whole bunch of people and you didn't know what to do about it.

ED:

What a bizarre memory you have.

AL:

I am right?

ED:

Right you are. And, this fellow just happened to be in Brooklyn and just happened to go into Hy's drugstore and somehow knew the tie-up between us and accidentally mentioned that I was more actor than Jew.

AL:

That's fantastic. Or, it's perfectly natural.

ED:

Take your choice.

AL:

You don't think I . . .

ED:

Listen, I have thought and thought and thought. I give up on it.

AL:

The only healthy thing to do.

ED:

You don't believe that faggot was balling Sandy and two years later decided to avenge some small slight.

AL:

I wouldn't put it past him.

ED:

I wouldn't put it past Sandy.

AL:

Come on, Ed. You can't tell me you expect perfect fidelity. You wouldn't have married a ballsy broad like Sandy.

ED:

How do you feel about Jane grabbing every and all males regardless of age, color or religious persuasion?

AL:

Shows my new-found maturity.

ED *laughs*.

She'll get over it. I'll bet you're laughing out of embarrassment.

ED:

I'm laughing but don't ask me why.

AL:

I mean I know about you and Jane. That's all right, Ed. She's only trying to get back at me. Perfectly natural.

ED:

Wait a minute.

AL:

You don't have to apologize, Ed. I understand. Look, what would you do if you had worked in one pressure box of an office after another for years and years. And your husband didn't work at all. You'd resent it. It's only natural. Then your old man gets a show and sells well. Not as much money as some think, but after all that time something. The next thing you know he leaves you. What do you think? Another woman. It's got to be another woman. It can't be that last great argument because that didn't happen at all. So it must be another chick. And when there is no other chick, then they really boil and fume. So don't be embarrassed. I understand.

ED:

I'll bet you'll never believe me when I tell you I have never made it with Jane.

AL:

I don't believe you.

ED:

Carry it to your grave. You can't fool me, you're covering. You didn't divorce Jane, she divorced you. You wouldn't commit yourself to any action. I think you couldn't bear living with someone who knew all your faults. You wanted to start a new life with the dough you got and who needed Jane to hamper your new fantasies. So you slopped around until Jane had to make the decision for both of you.

AL:

That's possible.

SARAH:

(*Off-stage*)

I'm home. I'm home.

(*Enters*)

Hi, Al. How are you? Sandy died. Did you hear? I'm staying with Daddy. Everything's turning out for the best. We'll be all right.

ED:

Didn't Grandma and Grandpa pick you up at school?

SARAH:

Yes, they went to the delicatessen. Grandma says you're a scarecrow. Grandpa gave me vitamins for you. Hey, whatever happened to your mother and father?

ED:

I've told you many times. My mother and father are dead.

SARAH:

Grandma says your mother is still alive. When are you going to get married again?

ED:

(*Gives* SARAH *paper and pencils*)

Why don't you draw in your room?

SARAH *exits*.

AL:

You know, I just realized that you must blame

yourself for Sandy's death, because you walked out on her.

Pause.

I guess you are a little bit to blame. If you had been around she might have lived a few hours more, huh?

ED:

I'm not a doctor.

AL:

That's right. You're a schoolteacher.

ED:

Are you trying to make me angry?

AL:

They say it's very good for someone in grief. Shocks them out of it.

ED:

(*Laughs*)
We get the friends we deserve.

AL:

That's something I always say. Now if I would have said it you'd have given me an argument.

ED:

You're probably right.

AL:

And I think I know why I come around here and get insulted all the time.

ED:

Now you've got me. Why?

AL:

Because you're no threat to me. Gee, that bothered me for a long time.

ED:

Was it a secret?

HY *and* SALLY *enter from auditorium.*

AL:

That must be your in-laws. I'd better go.

ED:

No, no. Please do me a favor and stick around for awhile.

SARAH *re-enters.*

SALLY:

I'll fix us a nice spread.

ED:

I'm not very hungry.

SALLY *and* SARAH *exit.*

HY:

Who's hungry? She's got to keep busy. I don't like to give advice, but that's not a bad piece. Keep busy.

ED:

I taught six classes today.

AL:

That must have been something else.

HY:

An ordeal, but wise. Yes, I think it was wise.

ED:

They didn't know anything about Sandy.

AL:

Didn't you say anything?

ED:

No, I intended to but I couldn't get it in.

HY:

I understand. Grief is private.

AL:

Do you plan to move out of here?

ED:

With what? Are you kidding?

HY:

No arguments please. Money is no problem. We trust you, Ed. You are a brave father. I want you to know that.

ED:

Thanks. I—

HY:

I come from a family of fourteen children. There are six of us left now. Four were born in the old country. Samuel, my father, was the first in his family to come to America. Then he sent for his sister but she took the wrong boat and went to Brazil instead. I think we have relatives there to this day. His brother Isaac came. He wasn't married then. And then two more brothers, rabbis I think, but they died within the first year here without ever speaking a word of English.

SALLY:

(*Entering*)
It'll be ready—

HY:

I'm talking about my family.

SALLY:

Oh, I'm sorry.
(*Exits with* AL)

HY:

Where was I? My father had five brothers and two sisters. The other sister never got to America either. She had syphilis, I've been told. Who knows? They say on her wedding night her husband ran off with the dowry. My grandfather was a horse thief. They were all horse thieves then. They came to America and then went back to be wiped out by the Nazis. They lived a long time only to be exterminated when nearly a hundred. The children of Isaac, there are four cousins, were Aaron, Bessie, Benjamin and little Toni. All dead now. Aaron committed suicide. He believed he would be insane like the rest of the children for their father married a first cousin. My Uncle Abe had six children and died smiling because they made him very proud. I remember seeing him the day he died. Nice man. Always had a kind word for everyone. He used to give me nickels and tell me to save them to go to college. His children weren't as nice as he thought. Sidney is an anti-Semite Republican in Cleveland. Esther, poor darling, has been in and out of mental institutions for twenty years. Sarah married a goy and wouldn't give us the time of day. Childless. That was God's vengeance. But Albert, the youngest, is blessed. Give—that's all that boy knew how to do. His father would have been proud of him. My Uncle Mordecai never married but it was rumored that he had a lot of bastard children. I never met him. He traveled in pots and pans. My father got a letter from him thirty years ago asking for help and never another letter. Uncle Sol had three engineers and they supported him in his old age. Although it wasn't always that way. The youngest ran off to the first World War and was reported missing for two years. Jake the oldest ran away for nine years. He was in Cincinnati all that time married and with wonderful children, Sandy used to play with them. He always told how he was too embarrassed to come home. One day a cousin saw him on the street and they both began crying in the middle of downtown Cincinnati. That's when he moved back to New York.

(*Cries a little*)

It was my time, not hers. God, it was my time—I'm old enough to have had my life. Why wasn't it me?

SARAH:

> (*Entering*)
> Let's eat! Let's eat! Let's eat!

SALLY:

> (*Entering with* AL)
> I'm sorry, Hy. I'm sorry, the child—

HY:

> That's all right. We should eat a little.

SARAH:

> Hurry! Hurry! I'm starving.

AL:

> I think I'd better go.

HY:

> You must eat something.

SALLY:

> You're not leaving without eating. Oh, no, I've made a corned beef sandwich with mayonnaise special for you, Al.

All attack the sandwiches and drinks rapaciously. Compliments on the food are shouted. Admissions of hunger are belted out. They begin to laugh and shout at each other.

Lights out. Cast exits. Slides of giant sandwiches and other food are shown on side panels with musical accompaniment.

Scene Two

A hospital room.

SANDY *in bed.* JANE *enters.*

SANDY:

How did you sneak in?

JANE:

I didn't. I told them I was a city inspector. Hey, am I glad to see you. I heard the news this morning. You are all right. I mean if you look all right why are you on the critical list?

SANDY:

I don't know. Am I? I may have to have an operation. They don't know yet. Maybe they put everyone on the critical list when they are about to have an operation.

JANE:

(*Taking off her coat and settling*)
Have you heard the one about the Jewish actor who drops dead in Oshkosh?

SANDY:

No.

JANE:

In the middle of a performance, this Jewish actor drops dead and the stage manager comes out and says "I'm very sorry, but Mr. Schwartz has expired." From the balcony a voice yells "Give him an enema." Then the stage manager explains "I'm very sorry but I think you've misunderstood me. I said Mr. Schwartz is dead, and an enema wouldn't help." And the reply was "It wouldn't hurt."

SANDY:

That was tactful.

JANE:

Oh, Jesus, I forgot you were sick. You won't die, Sandy, come on, you're just scaring me.

SANDY:

Nothing scares you.

JANE:

Why are you bugged with me? I've just spent the better part of two hours sneaking in here because I like you.

SANDY:

Cut it out, Jane. I don't know why you are here. I couldn't care less. I am glad you are but that doesn't blind me. Anyway, I'm still bugged with the way in which you're treating Al. You should be furious.

JANE:

But why? It's my business. I'm just not going to let him get my goat. That's all. As a matter of fact, I took Luis home just to piss him off.

SANDY:

Luis?

JANE:

Ed's student. Don't you know him very well?

SANDY:

I met him the same time you did.

JANE:

Oh. That's funny.

SANDY:

You should have gotten something out of it besides more trouble. Money. Something.

JANE:

I got all he could give. I'm sorry about not getting any dough, too. But what am I going to do? Change Al?

SANDY:

Has he got anything besides money? Oh, I'm just irritable. Forget it.

JANE:

I don't mind talking about it. My theory is that you want me to react to life the way you would.

SANDY:

That's true enough. I don't want to see any woman make the martyr scene.

JANE:

I'm not a—listen, I didn't come here to get you upset. Let's drop it.

SANDY:

Let's face it. As soon as you get onto something you

don't want to think about you want to drop it.

JANE:

What's wrong with being a martyr? Big deal. Where would the world be if we didn't have a few martyrs?

SANDY:

Is Al impotent?

JANE:

Not that I can remember. Why? Do you want me to send him up. He's a living doll. Is Ed impotent? What kind of question is that?

SANDY:

Just curious. That's all.

JANE:

Horseshit. Just curious, I'll bet. I wouldn't doubt that he's come on to you. Don't tell me you've fallen for him, too.

SANDY:

(*Getting out of bed*)
What do you mean?

JANE:

Well, recently, there's been some pretty models just dying to know about art and Al used to bring them up for coffee. Al tells them all about it. No, I mean I'm pretty sure that's all there is to it. But then I know better, don't I? He's good-looking. I don't blame them.

SANDY:

I guess I don't qualify.

JANE:

Shouldn't you stay in bed? I mean, you are sick.

SANDY:

I feel weak. Not too bad.

JANE:

What is it exactly?

SANDY:

I'm not a doctor. They don't know for sure. Something strange in the lower tract. God, how little they know. How little they tell you.

JANE:

Who's your doctor? Do you trust him?

SANDY:

I don't know him. He comes around with a dozen students or specialists and jokes.

Pause.

Why don't we give him and his crew a run for their money. You get into bed and let's see what he does then.

JANE:

You're not serious.

SANDY:

Certainly. I am very serious. It's all so impersonal. My doctor won't know the difference. Let's scien-

tifically test him. I'll bet he gives you a grave
diagnosis. Besides, you must give a dying man his
last wish.

JANE:

How could you be dying and joke like that? Gee,
you're always kidding me.

SANDY:

He's due here any minute. Come on.
(*Gets a white gown for Jane*)
Where's your sense of humor? In bed, come on.

JANE:

Where do I hurt?

SANDY:

Nothing really painful. Be evasive.

JANE:

He's going to get very angry.

Enter DOC.

DOC:

Did I hear the word angry?
(*To* JANE)
You are a very sick woman and I won't have
other patients bothering you. If you—
(*To* SANDY)
Will you please leave us.
(*Examines* JANE)

SANDY:

I'm sorry, doctor. I'm Mrs. Stone. It was just a

stupid game I was going to play on you. I'm sorry.

DOC:

Oh, God, ladies' pranks. Well, let's get you in bed.

JANE:

(*Taking off gown*)
Sandy, I—I had so many things I wanted to talk about.

SANDY:

Don't go. I'm sure the doctor isn't that mean.

DOC:

I'm afraid that he is. I must insist on your friend leaving. This is a hospital, not a hotel. I've got a hell of a lot of work and very little time to do it in and that's that.

SANDY:

Well, take care of your other patients and see me on your way back.

JANE:

Pause.

Really, Sandy, I wanted to tell you so—I can't think now. Isn't that funny? I had them all listed in my mind on the way up, A, B, C. Now—I'm sorry, doctor, I'll go now. When can I see you again?

SANDY:

Ask stoneface.

DOC:

Check with the front desk.

JANE:

(*Almost crying*)
Good-bye, Sandy.
(*Exits*)

SANDY:

My God, I'm not dead yet.

DOC:

Close to it.

SANDY:

Are you trying to scare me?

DOC:

Yes.

SANDY:

Okay. I'm scared. Now what?

DOC:

You need an operation.

SANDY:

That's very expensive treatment. How much is all
this surgery going to cost? My husband's a schoolteacher.

DOC:

I'll discuss the fee with him.

SANDY:

Are you doing this because it's really necessary or
are you just running up the bill?

DOC:

Do you actually think I'd suggest surgery merely to make a buck?

SANDY:

Of course. Don't all doctors do that?

DOC:

(*Sits. Laughs*)
Was that girl a good friend of yours?

SANDY:

No. Why? Do you want her phone number?

DOC:

No, I've plenty of nurses right here in the hospital. You know what they say about doctors. They're all unscrupulous and they have plenty of nurses—aside from being wealthy in the extreme, good-looking and addicted to drugs.

SANDY:

Actually, Jane and I are not close. It's just that she thinks I've slept with her husband—and I know my husband has slept with her.

DOC:

Oh, I see. That makes sense. That clears it up.

SANDY:

Stop putting me on. You're not very good at it.

DOC:

Neither are you.

SANDY:

I'm telling the truth, Charlie.

DOC:

Of that I have no doubt. However, when I walked in I did have the impression that you girls were in bed together and that's why I asked about your relationship.

SANDY:

You thought we were Lesbians?

DOC:

I honestly did for a minute.

SANDY *laughs.*

It's all in a day's work. It might easily have been that.

SANDY:

Don't let me interrupt your rounds.

DOC:

I say let's play a game. You be the patient and I'll be the doctor. You like it so far? It's the only game I know. I'll try to heal you and you try to be healed. Fair enough? Now, do you see an analyst? or psychotherapist?

SANDY:

Yes, when I can afford it. Does it show?

DOC:

How long have you had treatment?

SANDY:

I get the impression I'm being interrogated at police headquarters.

Pause.

On and off for about three years.

Pause.

We Lesbians need to be straightened out.

DOC:

Your husband's a lucky fellow. You're a brave and funny girl. I wouldn't worry too much. It'll ruin your beautiful complexion.

SANDY:

I feel very unfunny and scared. Thanks for the flattery. When can I have visitors?

DOC:

We'll discuss that after the operation.

SANDY:

And if I don't recover?

DOC:

Will you stop it! Okay, let's say you don't recover. We all die alone anyway. Relax. It's not all that complicated. Ring the bell for the nurse and ask for a TV set, books, orange juice, cosmetics, anything.

SANDY:

Hey, what do you think this is? A hotel? By the way, what is wrong with me?

DOC:

It's too technical to explain.

SANDY:

I'll bet you say that to all your patients.

DOC:

Just the pretty ones . . .

SANDY:

I want to know. I'm not dumb.

DOC:

It's a similar operation to the one Eisenhower had. Remember?

SANDY:

The nose bob?

DOC:

Ever the joker. No, a little snip of a piece of tubing.

SANDY:

Just something to do with my ileum or colon. That's all?

DOC:

We don't know the exact conditions we'll find.

SANDY:

Oh, you're going to do an exploratory.

DOC:

Well, yes. The tests have been running in that direction.

SANDY:

What about my ovaries?

DOC:

Generally—

SANDY:

I don't want to hear what happens generally.

DOC:

As I was saying, generally speaking there shouldn't be any cause for concern. I can't discuss this any further with you.

SANDY:

What's all this business about my analyst?

DOC:

I really should be on my way.

SANDY:

What kind of examination is this? Aren't you going to take my pulse?

DOC:

Pause.

No thanks.

SANDY:

Are you afraid to touch me?

DOC:

Not at all. As long as you're under anesthesia.

SANDY:

Wait until the AMA hears about that.

DOC:

I believe you're a little too much for me this morning.
(*Exits*)

SANDY:

Pause.

What's his hurry? He was afraid of me. No doubt about it. I wonder if they would bury me alive? No. No. I wanted to ask him so much more. God, he was cocky. I certainly wanted to cut him down. You speck of dandruff in the wind. Listen, Doc, don't you know that our sun is only one of hundreds of thousands? And it won't last forever either. Doesn't astronomy awe you? Does nothing awe you? Oh, I'm sorry. You are impressed with other kinds of things. Glandular transplants. Yes, very awe-inspiring. Hope they work. Ha, ha, ha. Don't experiment with me.

Pause, then long fog horn.

God, I wish I had a Vogue or something. Something with pictures.

Enter HY *with packages.*

Pop!

HY:

A sweater? Here.
(*Counts out some money*)

No, you want another suit?
(*Counts out more money*)

SANDY:

You don't understand, Pop. This is it. I'm gone.
There's no second chance.

HY:

I forgive you everything. Here!
(*Counts more money*)
I'll name a research wing in a famous hospital after
you. You name it.

SANDY:

Take care of Momma. She's not going to take the
news well.

HY:

You always were a little meshugana. Sally will love
every tear, every sob. Besides, who says you have
to go?
(*Counts out a lot more money*)

SALLY:

(*Enters with food*)
If you got to go, go. But, here's a little something.
Don't tell me you're not hungry. Eat.

SARAH:

(*Entering*)
Hi, Mommie. Read to me like you used to.

SANDY:

I'm tired, honey.

HY:

   She's tired.

SALLY:

   She's tired.

BILL, JR.:

   (*Entering*)
   Hey, Mom. I hear you're tired. It's your own fault.
   I wish you were dead. How could you have married
   Ed? Baaaah!

HY:

   You kids leave your mother alone.
   (*Hands out money to them*)
   Buy yourself a little something.

SALLY:

   So why should the children starve? We all can't
   be good cooks. Somebody has to do the cooking
   now that Sandy's gone. We can't all be demonstra-
   tors for peace.

SANDY:

   Get out. All of you get out and leave me alone.

Pushes them out: HY *still handing out money,* SALLY
eating and the children noisy. Silence.

   Ladies, we are gathered here to do the job most men
   shun thinking about. We are going to plot against
   the idiots who want to blow up the world with their
   nuclear toys.

Cheers.

What do they care that they are poisoning generations to come?

More cheers.

Women, stand up now and fight.

More cheers. ED *enters.*

ED:

Why the shouting? A test ban agreement has been reached.

SANDY:

All right, what about the DDT in our food?

More cheers.

What about the utilities monopolies?

More cheers.

High prices?

Cheers.

Poverty?

Cheers.

What about funeral practices in America?

Cheers.

Civil rights?

Very loud cheers.

Are we going to be lulled into complacency?

Cries of "No!"

This time we'll go after the big one. We're going all out against the double standard.

Cries of "Oooooh."

Yes, I know it's hard to believe. It's not going to be easy. We've had some success in the past. Let's not let it go to our head. This is the time to strike and strike fast.

ED:

You and your eternal battle of the sexes. I've been hitting the sack with you for years and I'll give you an unequivocal recommendation.

SANDY:

None of your sarcasm, Ed. You think you can wipe out our work with a sneer. Uh-uh. No sir. Don't give me your usual old cover-up story. We all know you're not a painter. We're the strong ones, Ed. Look around, Charlie, they all agree with me. Hey, Luis!

LUIS:

(Entering)

I'd just like to say that living with Jane Jaafe has made a new person out of me. I know that it has forever cut me off from my old friends and relatives. My mother and father never had my best interests at heart for they had to look after themselves first and I'm the first to sympathize. Now nothing could be more natural than for them to hate me for what they consider my immoral acts.

Naturally, they think it is very bad for me to be living with Jane. Of course, being a petty thief or a dope addict would be for them a much better scene. I now have a sense of responsibility which may seem somewhat ironic. I don't ask that everyone understand or follow in my footsteps. Thank you.

(*Exits*)

SANDY:

How do you like that, Ed? Where's your sarcasm now?

Cheers.

The apparatus of representative government needs revision. We must lead the fight in making our country aware.

Cheers into:

AL:

(*Entering*)

You know, not very long ago I discovered that I was impotent. I discussed this rather personal problem with just about every pretty young girl that I met. I know I should have included a great many more older women for statistical purposes but opportunities did not present themselves. Pretty girls have a special talent for trying to help a fellow with my kind of problem. And I'm here to pay tribute to each and every one. Special mention needs to be made of Mrs. Sandra Stone of New York City

who, beyond the call of friendship, straightened
out a few of my kinks.
(*Pins medal on* SANDY *and kisses her*)
We all salute you!

Cheers while AL *exits.* BILL, JR. *enters.*

BILL, JR.:

I demand a trial. Let her burn!

ED:

(*To* SANDY)
You'll just have to bear this. They can't help themselves.

SARAH:

Call your first witness.
(*Grabbing* ED)
Oh, sweetie!

ED:

Don't call on me. Call her parents.

HY *and* SALLY *enter.*

BILL, JR.:

Take the witness stand, please. Now when did you
first notice—

SALLY:

The first time she married. That's when I first no-
ticed it. There were other times—

SANDY:

What am I accused of?

SARAH:

Come off it. You weren't a very good mother in the standard sense of the word. You couldn't cook. You couldn't sew. You couldn't—what's the use, I admit it: I didn't like the way you took daddy away.

BILL, JR.:

This is ridiculous. As president I demand we try to make sense out of nonsense. I want order. I want it more than anything. Continue!

HY:

Billy, I'll buy you anything. Just don't scream.

SALLY:

Anything.

SANDY:

That's exactly what they said to me, Billy. Don't be bribed, my Billy. It costs too much.

BILL, JR.:

I'm not on trial here. I didn't commit your indiscretions. Let's follow the procedure, mother, at least once in your life. I wouldn't give advice if I were you. Look at where you ended up.

SANDY:

I raised that!

ED:

I helped a little.

SARAH:

Oh, Ed, don't falter. Let's get this over with so we can burn her and get on to other things.

HY:

I ought to explain. It's really my fault. I should have taken the prospective husband to one side and said—my daughter's not well, you're taking a big chance. You see, Sandy has been imperfect since childhood. Then everything would have been fair. And fair is fair.

SARAH:

That doesn't matter. She gave up religion.

BILL, JR.:

And she didn't even trouble herself about our religious training. Let's stop talking and burn her.

SALLY:

I warned you what would happen when you turn away.

BILL, JR.:

Are there any more witnesses?

ED:

Certainly.

AL:

(*Entering*)
She let me down. I want to string up the little vixen.

SANDY:

But, Al, you already testified—

BILL, JR.:

Can I have order among you so-called adults?

AL:

I know it's perjury. Hell, I got the whole thing so confused in my mind I could testify to anything. In any event I want to see a real martyr. If you've never seen a real one you ain't lived.

ED:

You don't think future generations are going to immortalize—

AL:

I don't think. I know. Sandy, you aren't mad, are you? We can disagree and still be friends.

SANDY:

If you're not with me, you are aginme.

BILL, JR.:

Will everyone stop blabbing, I'm close to a mystical experience which will tell me the answer.

JANE:

(*Entering*)

I'd like to say a few words in defense of my good friend, Sandy—

ED:

We all know how jealous you are of Sandy and therefore your testimony can't be admitted.

JANE:

Oh, Ed, let me take you away from all this.

SANDY:

Get her out of here. I can defend myself.

JANE *exits.*

BILL, JR.:

This is your last chance before my mystical experience. What do you have to say for yourself?

SANDY:

I want to admit that I have consciously withheld religious instruction from my children.

Taped boos.

I am a lousy housekeeper.

Booing.

I can't sew or cook.

Booing.

So what? I have no need to defend myself. Those jobs are for servants.

SARAH *boos weakly.*

Yet, there was only a faint hope it would ever be otherwise. I needed that more than anything else. I think I know why you are even bothering with me. You know I can help you. First, you get me to submit and then let me off by asking my help. I know all of your tricks, Ed. You know mine too.

If only I had a career instead of children or before I had children. Oh, Ed, you could never sell a painting. God, I wish you didn't rely on my selecting the valuable ones. Why did I ever get myself in that position? Who wants to be a critic? Who needed to schlepp your stuff around? I knew it was horrible for you so I did it. Now what'll happen to you, Ed? Who will carry them? Who will throw out all the garbage that you do? That stuff that blinds you so that you can't tell whether it's any good or not. Oh, God, I hope you find someone who isn't bowled over with you and who will swear at you and tear at you. It'll be just your luck to marry some vapid rich doll and her docility will be the death of Ed Stone, the painter. Oh, Sarah, how did you fit into my high heel shoes?

SARAH *cries*.

Cry and cry. Don't be cheated out of mourning just because you can't stand the hypocrisy of the other mourners. You'll regret not crying. Mother, take her away.

SALLY *exits with* SARAH.

Now I've got the men all to myself. For Christ's sake, Billy, stop playing judge. I know children are supposed to run their families and all that. I know I'm not a good mother in the old-fashioned sense. I'm still your mother and get off it before I spank the living daylights out of you. Uh, uh,

Billy. Don't make a fool of yourself. Keep your mouth shut and get out. Pop?

HY *exits with* BILLY.

I hope he turns out well. They say all boys go through this arrogant, conservative phase. I hope he gets through it and onto something a little more ambitious than being a bank teller.

BILL, JR.:
(*Off-stage*)
Cost Accountant!

SANDY:
Oh, how I loved school. I missed my calling. I should have become a schoolteacher. Like you, Ed. Yes, you never thought you'd hear me say it. It's true. Having children isn't enough. If I could have been a key, a door, a catalyst as my teachers were, then I wouldn't have this dreaded emptiness inside me now. Well, it's some comfort to have figured it out. Oh, Ed, I can't stop talking.

ED:
Shhh . . .

They kiss and ED *starts to exit through auditorium.*

ON TAPE

ED: "Shhh . . ."
SANDY: "What are you going to do?"

ED: "I'll find someone. Get married. Take care of Sarah. Try."

(ED *is gone*.)

SANDY: "I love you Ed."

ED: "I got all caught up in it. I don't want to bug you now."

SANDY: "Don't go— Don't Ed."